Watch an Orange Grow

by Kirsten Chang

Bullfrog Books

Ideas for Parents and Teachers

Bullfrog Books let children practice reading informational text at the earliest reading levels. Repetition, familiar words, and photo labels support early readers.

Before Reading

- Discuss the cover photo. What does it tell them?

- Look at the picture glossary together. Read and discuss the words.

Read the Book

- "Walk" through the book and look at the photos. Let the child ask questions. Point out the photo labels.

- Read the book to the child, or have him or her read independently.

After Reading

- Prompt the child to think more. Ask: Do you like to eat oranges? Can you explain how they grow?

Bullfrog Books are published by Jump!
5357 Penn Avenue South
Minneapolis, MN 55419
www.jumplibrary.com

Library of Congress Cataloging-in-Publication Data

Names: Chang, Kirsten, author.
Title: Watch an orange grow / by Kirsten Chang.
Description: Minneapolis, MN: Jump!, Inc., [2019]
Series: Watch it grow | Audience: Age 5–8.
Audience: K to Grade 3. | Includes index.
Identifiers: LCCN 2018026420 (print)
LCCN 2018026929 (ebook)
ISBN 9781641282758 (ebook)
ISBN 9781641282734 (hardcover: alk. paper)
ISBN 9781641282741 (paperback)
Subjects: LCSH: Oranges—Growth
—Juvenile literature.
Classification: LCC SB370.O7 (ebook)
LCC SB370.O7 C43 2019 (print) | DDC 634/.31—dc23
LC record available at https://lccn.loc.gov/2018026420

Editor: Jenna Trnka
Designer: Michelle Sonnek

Photo Credits: Iryna Denysova/Shutterstock, cover; arka38/Shutterstock, 1, 8–9 (foreground), 13, 17, 22tr, 22br, 22tl, 23tm, 23bl, 23br; Palokha Tetiana/Shutterstock, 3; Nachaphon/Shutterstock, 4 (foreground); Sukpaiboonwat/Shutterstock, 4 (background); Vassev/Shutterstock, 5; ekkapon/Shutterstock, 6, 22t; Anamar/Shutterstock, 6–7; Roxana Bashyrova/Shutterstock, 8–9 (background), 22tr, 23bl, 23br; Marco Ossino/Shutterstock, 10–11; Olegusk/Shutterstock, 12; Design Pics Inc/Alamy, 14–15, 22bl, 23tl; Segen/Shutterstock, 16; hanapon1002/Shutterstock, 18–19; wavebreakmedia/Shutterstock, 20–21; Filipe B. Varela/Shutterstock, 23tr; GalapagosPhoto/Shutterstock, 23bm; Maks Narodenko/Shutterstock, 24.

Printed in the United States of America at Corporate Graphics in North Mankato, Minnesota.

Table of Contents

Ripe Fruit

Jon loves to eat oranges.

How do they grow?

An orange starts
as a seed.

The seed is planted
in warm soil.

It needs water.

seed

seedling

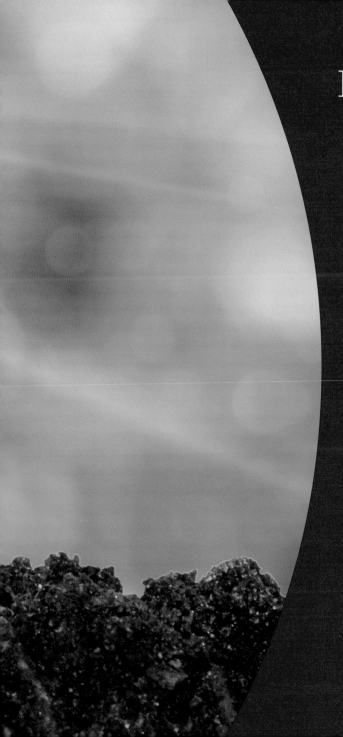

It grows into
a seedling.

It has roots
and a stem.

Leaves collect
sunlight.

9

The plant grows
into a small tree.

The tree
needs water.

Orange trees need sunlight.

Years go by.

The tree grows.

In spring,
flowers bloom.

The flowers grow into fruit.
At first, the fruit is green.

It ripens.
It turns orange.

In fall, they are
ready to pick.

We pick them
by hand.

18

We can buy them
at the store, too.

We love oranges!

Life Cycle of an Orange

How does an orange grow?

seed

seedling

tree

flowers

orange

Picture Glossary

bloom
To produce flowers.

ripens
Becomes ready
to eat.

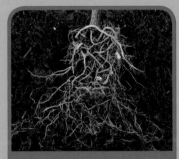

roots
Parts of a plant that
grow underground
and get water and
food from the soil.

seedling
A young plant
grown from a seed.

soil
Another word
for dirt.

stem
The long, thin
part of a plant
that grows leaves.

Index

To Learn More

Learning more is as easy as 1, 2, 3.

1) Go to www.factsurfer.com

2) Enter "watchanorangegrow" into the search box.

3) Click the "Surf" button to see a list of websites.

With factsurfer.com, finding more information is just a click away.